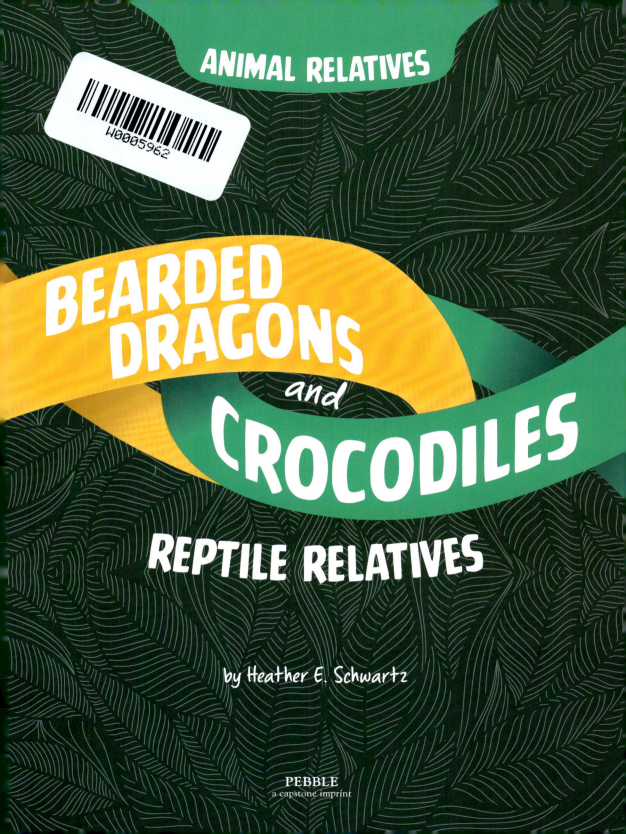

ANIMAL RELATIVES

BEARDED DRAGONS and CROCODILES

REPTILE RELATIVES

by Heather E. Schwartz

PEBBLE
a capstone imprint

Published by Pebble, an imprint of Capstone
1710 Roe Crest Drive, North Mankato, Minnesota 56003
capstonepub.com

Copyright © 2026 by Capstone. All rights reserved. No part of this publication may be reproduced in whole or in part, or stored in a retrieval system, or transmitted in any form or by any means, electronic, mechanical, photocopying, recording, or otherwise, without written permission of the publisher.

Library of Congress Cataloging-in-Publication Data
is available on the Library of Congress website.

ISBN: 9798875220166 (hardcover)
ISBN: 9798875220111 (paperback)
ISBN: 9798875220128 (ebook PDF)

Summary: Are crocodiles and bearded dragons actually related? Readers will investigate how these reptile relatives are alike and different in terms of habitats, life cycles, senses and defenses, and other characteristics.

Editorial Credits
Editor: Ashley Kuehl; Designer: Bobbie Nuytten; Media Researcher: Svetlana Zhurkin; Production Specialist: Whitney Schaefer

Image Credits
Getty Images: Ayzenstayn, 28, CamiloTorres, 20, Dmitri Korobtsov, 25, Fotografer Garuda, 6, John Elk III, 29, John W. Banagan, 12, Ken Griffiths, 11, lessydoang, 23; Shutterstock: Anton_Ivanov, 9, Barbie Lewis, 15, Decha Photography, 8, Jaime Nicolau, 7, JMx Images, 18, mr_tigga, 5, Nick Greaves, 17, Ocimadfoto, 16, Paco Como, 10, Pepi M Firmansyah, 13, 27, PinkeshTanna, 24, Serhii Shcherbyna, 21, Stu Porter, 19, suriyachan, cover (top), TamamaB, 22, tritangguh99, cover (bottom), Twins Design Studio (background), cover, 1, 30, viveraphoto, 4

Any additional websites and resources referenced in this book are not maintained, authorized, or sponsored by Capstone. All product and company names are trademarks™ or registered® trademarks of their respective holders.

TABLE OF CONTENTS

Same or Different? 4

A Closer Look 6

Best Behavior 10

Home Sweet Home 14

Mealtime 18

Creature Communication 22

Feeling Friendly 26

    Can You Remember? 30

    Animal Jokes 30

    Glossary 31

    Index 32

    About the Author 32

Words in **bold** are in the glossary.

SAME OR DIFFERENT?

Have you ever seen a bearded dragon? How about a crocodile? They look a bit alike. And they do have something in common. Both are reptiles. But bearded dragons are lizards. Crocodiles are not. They are related to birds!

What else makes these animals alike and different? Let's find out!

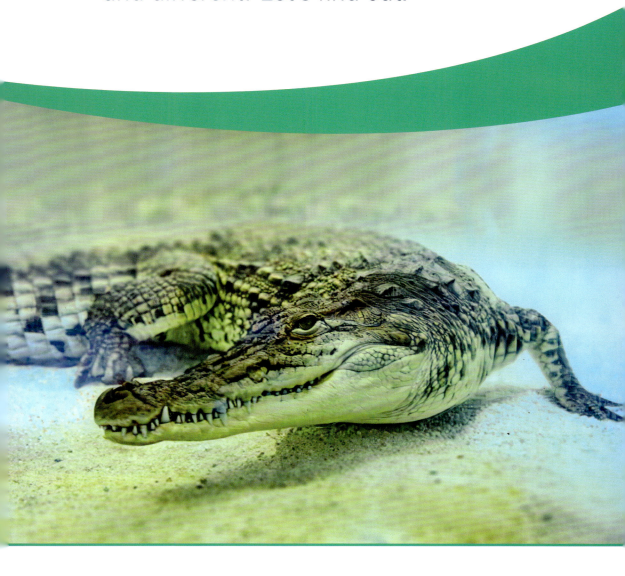

A CLOSER LOOK

These two reptiles have different kinds of bodies. Crocodiles are bigger. **Hatchlings** are about 1 foot (0.3 meter) long. Adults can grow to 20 feet (6 m) long. Some weigh as much as a car!

FUN FACT

The saltwater crocodile is the biggest reptile in the world!

Bearded dragons are much smaller. Hatchlings are about 3 inches (7.6 centimeters) long. Adults grow up to 24 inches (61 cm) long. And they're easy to pick up too. They are as light as a loaf of bread!

Some parts of their bodies look alike too. Both animals have scaly skin. But they come in different colors. Bearded dragons can be brown or tan. They can be red, orange, yellow, or white. They are best known for their beard. It is made of spikes.

Crocodiles have a gray and green back. They have a white and yellow belly. They are famous for their long **snout**. It is filled with large, sharp teeth.

BEST BEHAVIOR

Do these animals act the same? Not really. Crocodiles hide in the water. They sink below the surface. Only their eyes, ears, **nostrils**, and the top of their head show from the shore. What a sneaky way to watch for **prey**!

Bearded dragons use their beard to stay safe. The beard puffs out when the animal feels scared. This helps scare off **predators**.

Neither animal sweats. But both need to beat the heat. Crocodiles sometimes act like people. They find a shady spot out of the sun. They crawl in the water for a swim.

FUN FACT

Sometimes crocodiles let out body heat by opening their mouths.

Bearded dragons try something different. They change color! The lizard's back may turn yellow. That means it's trying to cool down. The light color **reflects** heat rays.

HOME SWEET HOME

A bearded dragon needs a tank. It needs help to feel at home. Heat lamps and lights make it warm enough. Branches and rocks give a lizard a place to climb. A hideaway spot is good for sleeping.

A clean tank is good for bearded dragons. But direct sunlight and loud noises are bad.

FUN FACT

Tank life is more fun with toys. Many bearded dragons enjoy toys made for cats.

Wild crocodiles live in warm places around the world. They make their homes in water. They live in swamps, lakes, rivers, and ponds.

When the weather is dry, they hide. They dig dens in the mud. They spend months sleeping in their dens. They come out when the rain returns again.

MEALTIME

Crocodiles are hunters. They hunt in the water. They hunt on the shore. They eat meat. And they find plenty of tasty treats in their natural **habitat**.

Babies snack on bugs and spiders. They eat frogs, snails, and snakes too. Adults dine on fish and turtles. They even eat large animals. Deer, pigs, and zebra are all on the menu. Crocodiles can make a meal of almost any creature.

FUN FACT

Crocodiles can survive for months without food or water.

Bearded dragons are also hunters. They don't hunt big animals. They hunt bugs and worms. Babies and adults chase crickets and roaches.

Bearded dragons eat other things too. Adults eat some fruits. They enjoy apples and strawberries. They eat a lot of vegetables. They like carrots, peppers, and sweet potatoes.

CREATURE COMMUNICATION

Sometimes bearded dragons hiss. They have something to say. They're scared! But most of the time, they're silent. They use body language to "talk."

They twitch their tail when stressed. They wave their arms to give up in a fight. A bearded dragon bobs its head to send a strong message. It says, "Can you see who's in charge now? Me!"

Crocodiles have a lot to say too. They usually use their voices. They can make many different sounds. They squeak, grunt, and whistle. They growl, hiss, and roar. Some babies make a quacking sound.

Why do crocodiles make so much noise? Sometimes they are scared. Other times, they are calling to each other. They answer many sounds they hear in the wild. They even call back to humans who make crocodile sounds!

FEELING FRIENDLY

Who likes people? Bearded dragons do! They live alone in their tanks. But they hang out with humans. A bearded dragon can recognize you. It might sit on your lap. It might fall asleep on you. You can pet a bearded dragon. Some will beg for food. Some will walk on a leash!

Wild crocodiles are dangerous. But some in **captivity** are gentle. They may form friendships with people. But this is rare. It happens when people care for crocodiles. The animals get to know the people. They recognize them.

Friendly crocodiles let people pet them. They swim with people. They play with people. But you should never get close to a wild crocodile. That is not safe.

CAN YOU REMEMBER?

1. Which adult animal is heavier, a crocodile or a bearded dragon?
2. What do crocodiles like to eat?
3. What should a bearded dragon's tank have in it?
4. How do bearded dragons communicate with each other?
5. What might happen if you make crocodile sounds near crocodiles?

Check your answers at the bottom of page 31!

ANIMAL JOKES

What do you call a crocodile in a vest?
An investigator

What is a reptile's favorite movie?
The Lizard of Oz

What do you call a bearded dragon that's good at rapping?
A rap-tile

GLOSSARY

captivity (kap-TIV-i-tee)—places where animals live that are not natural habitats, such as zoos or aquariums

habitat (HAB-i-tat)—the home of an animal in the wild

hatchling (HACH-ling)—a baby crocodile

nostril (NAH-struhl)—the holes in an animal's snout used for breathing

predator (PRED-uh-tur)—an animal that hunts others

prey (PRAY)—an animal that is hunted for food

reflect (ri-FLEKT)—to throw back heat without absorbing it

snout (SNOUT)—the nose and mouth of an animal

1. A crocodile; 2. Animals, including fish, turtles, snails, snakes, or even deer, pigs, or zebra; 3. Heat lamps, rocks and branches, and a hiding place; 4. Using body language and sometimes hissing; 5. They might call back.

INDEX

beards, 8, 11
birds, 4
body language, 22–23

colors, 8–9, 13
communication, 22–25

food, 18–21, 26

heat, 12, 13, 14
homes, 14–17
hunting, 18–20

length, 6–7
lizards, 4, 13, 14

people, 12, 25, 26, 28–29

skin, 8
sounds, 22, 24–25

tanks, 14–15, 26

weight, 6–7

ABOUT THE AUTHOR

Heather E. Schwartz is an award-winning children's book author in upstate New York. She lives with her husband, two kids, and two cats named Stampy and Squid. In elementary school, her class kept small lizards called newts. She cared for them over vacation and tried to race them. They barely moved!